War Men

A Guide for Fami

SUSAN TALL

THE FAMILY HISTORY PARTNERSHIP

Published by
The Family History Partnership
57 Bury New Road, Ramsbottom
Bury, Lancashire BL0 0BZ

www.thefamilyhistorypartnership.com

First published 2014

Copyright © Susan Tall

ISBN: 978 1 906280 46 8

Printed and bound by
Berforts Information Press
Southfield Road, Eynsham
Oxford OX29 4JB

CONTENTS

ACKNOWLEDGEMENTS

Thanks to the members of the Family History Partnership especially Richard Ratcliffe who suggested I write this book, to Bob Boyd for all his practical help at the production stage, and to my husband, David, for preparing the text layout and processing the illustrations. The URL addresses are correct at the time of publication. Any errors and omissions are, of course, my own.

I would like to thank the following for permission to use their illustrations:

Peter Coulls, Offchurch St Gregory's font (p.15)
Alain Foote, Willans & Robinson memorial (p.23)
Warwickshire County Record Office for the photograph of Kenilworth Red Cross Hospital, ref C362 BVI, p.75 (p.55)
Page from the London Gazette covered by the Open Government Licence (p.49)
Kenilworth Advertiser (pp.11, 41)
Coventry Herald (p.41)

and the following for allowing me to take photographs of local memorials:

Kenilworth Post Office (p.11)
Kenilworth Working Men's Club (p.11)
Kenilworth St. Nicholas' Church (pp.11, 43)
Kenilworth St. Barnabas' Church. (p.25)

All other illustrations are my own.

PREFACE

I have always attended the Remembrance Day ceremony at our local war memorial in Kenilworth, Warwickshire and over the years had wondered who the people were whose names were listed on it. I had not been born in the town but had lived there long enough to recognise many of the names as local ones and wondered which families they belonged to, what jobs they did, and of course what part they played in war and how they met their deaths.

An opportunity to do something about it came when our local family history group were considering a millennium project and it was suggested we research the names on the town war memorial. I jumped at the chance to have a go at this. Five years later the book "Kenilworth and the Great War", written by myself and Betty Sunley, was produced, as well as a website which includes casualties from both world wars, **www.kenilworth-war-memorial.org.uk**. Nearly ten years later I'm still involved with researching these men, still learning new facts and am as fascinated by war memorials as ever.

This book should prove useful to both family and local historians. It is divided into two parts. The first looks at how you might locate a war memorial on which a family member or particular person is named. The second explains how to research that name and find out about a person's military history. Local historians may want to skip the first part of the book if they already have a war memorial in mind and just want to find out how to research the names. However if you are thinking of starting your own war memorial website you may find the ones referred to as useful examples.

Do your research carefully and, although you will often uncover sad and heart-breaking stories, by finding out about the people behind the names on war memorials, you can help make sure they are remembered by future generations.

INTRODUCTION

There are estimated to be over 100,000 war memorials in the United Kingdom. Some are well known landmarks such as the Cenotaph in London or the towering naval memorials in Plymouth, Portsmouth and Chatham, but for the most part war memorials blend into the general landscape of our towns and villages and largely go unnoticed by the general public. The majority of families, however, will have someone whose name has been inscribed on one, and, for the family historian, they can open up a whole new area of research and give an insight into the lives and military history of our ancestors.

War memorials come in all shapes and sizes, with many situated in places where we would not normally think of looking for them. They range from stone crosses and obelisks in villages and towns to memorial plaques, stained glass windows and fonts inside churches. There are buildings such as village memorial halls, institutes, reading rooms, school and university chapels as well as memorial parks, gardens and playing fields. Some are quite unusual. You can find benches, bus shelters, lych gates, clocks, lamps, fountains, horse troughs, even the whole lighting system for a church, all being used as memorials for those who died as a result of war. Sporting and social clubs often have their own memorials as do places of employment.

The history of war memorials is relatively short. It is only in modern times that memorials have been erected to commemorate those who died in wars rather than celebrating great victories in battle. The Wellington Monument in Somerset is a fine example of the latter, celebrating the Duke of Wellington's victory over Napoleon in the Battle of Waterloo in 1815. However, such a monument is of little interest to those researching war memorials as it does not include any information on those who fought and died.

A small number of memorials were erected for the Crimean War (1853-1856), a few of which have names on them, such as the one in Bath Abbey Cemetery, but it was only at the end of the 19th century that it became common for British Army regiments to build monuments to their comrades who had died in Imperial wars and to record their names.

The Wellington Monument in Somerset.

Following the Second Anglo-Boer War (1899-1902), in which many volunteers took part, some towns and cities in the UK raised funds to commemorate men from their communities who had fought and died. The pictures opposite show the Boer War Memorial in Winsford, Cheshire which lists not only the six men that died from the town, including their regiments and the places where they died, but also the volunteers and regular servicemen who fought for their country.

It was only after the great losses of the First World War that war memorials were erected in their thousands all over Britain. With the government's decision not to repatriate bodies, together with so many casualties having no known graves, the building of these memorials can be seen as a communal expression of grief as well as a practical solution to give relatives somewhere local they could visit and remember their loved ones who had died fighting for their country.

After the Second World War names of those who died were often added to these existing memorials, as they were again after the Korean War. More recently the UK National Memorial Arboretum in Staffordshire has been built and hosts the Armed Forces Memorial which displays the names of almost 16,000 service personnel who have lost their lives either in conflict, as a result of terrorism, or on training exercises since the end of the Second World War.

It is estimated there are 1.5 million names on war memorials throughout the United Kingdom.

The criteria for placing names on war memorials

There are no standard criteria for having a name on a war memorial. Local communities drew up lists of the fallen, mainly local councils or churches who were often reliant on relatives giving details. The next of kin may be a parent, a wife, a brother or sister, or another responsible adult, who may live in the same town or may have moved or lived elsewhere. It is therefore highly possible that some individuals will be listed on several different memorials or even on none at all. They may be on a national memorial as well as a town memorial, perhaps in a church where they worshipped, a school memorial, their workplace or a social club.

Winsford Boer War Memorial, unveiled 24th November, 1906

The Memorial today

Private James Harris, a postman from Kenilworth, who served with the 2nd South Staffordshire Regiment, is recorded on four memorials within the town: the main town memorial, the parish church memorial, the Post Office roll of honour, which is now displayed in the parcel office, and the Kenilworth Working Men's Club memorial. The majority of memorials list those who died in war, but there are many that list all the people from a certain parish, workforce or social club who went to fight for their country, whether they returned or not. The Kenilworth Working Men's Club memorial lists all of its members who served in the Great War with a central plaque for those who died. It is puzzling to find James Harris amongst those who served but not named amongst those who died. His name has been varnished over (at the foot of the second row of the list on the page opposite) as if it was realised that he had died but it was not possible to repaint the memorial to add his name to the shield in the middle.

There are even some memorials in places where all those who went off to war returned safely and these have been given the name "Thankful Villages". You can find out about the 53 World War One thankful villages, including 13 which are now considered to be "Double Thankful Villages", in that they lost no service personnel in the Second World War, at

www.hellfirecorner.co.uk/thankful.htm

Not all memorials have lists of names on them. In larger towns and cities, where there were too many names to inscribe on a memorial, you will often find a roll of honour usually in the form of a book or books of remembrance. These can be found in various places such as a nearby parish church or cathedral, the local library or archives, and increasingly on the internet.

PRIVATE J. HARRIS
(2nd South Staffordshires.)

Post Office Roll of Honour

Town War Memorial

St Nicholas Church Memorial (as **JAMES** Harris)

Working Men's Club War Memorial

A soldier may be on several different war memorials

11

HOW TO FIND IF A RELATIVE IS RECORDED ON A WAR MEMORIAL

It would be wonderful just to type your ancestor's name into a search engine and come up with the memorials they are listed on, but, although this may happen in the future, at the moment it is a question of searching all the different resources available and hoping to strike it lucky.

You may have heard family stories about granddad or a great uncle being killed in the war, so the most obvious place to start is the area where your relatives lived. If you can take a personal trip, have a look at all the war memorials in the vicinity, as your relative could be recorded on more than one memorial and there may be extra information on different memorials such as age, regiment, date of death and location. Look inside churches for memorial plaques or hand-written rolls of honour as well as churchyards and cemeteries as their names may have been added onto family headstones.

Before you start your research you should bear in mind the inconsistencies in the way names are recorded on war memorials, often making it quite difficult to identify whether it is your relative or not. Spellings of surnames can differ from one memorial to another and very often initials are changed around. This could be because someone was known locally by their middle name or a nickname. For example, William James Smith, who was known as James or Jimmy, may not always be recorded as W. J. Smith on a memorial, he may become J. W. Smith or just J. Smith. Whilst some memorials just have initials and a surname, others have a full first name and may include rank and regiment and even date and place of death.

There do not seem to be any hard and fast rules or regulations about how you record the names on a war memorial. The First World War memorial in Sandon, Staffordshire gives an amazing amount of information. On one panel (see opposite) as well as names it gives their rank and regiment, the date they died and where. It also divides the names up into killed in action, died of wounds or died. On a further panel it gives statistics with the number of those who joined the forces, those killed in action, died of

ROLL OF HONOUR

KILLED IN ACTION

MAJ. RYDER, HON. R.N.D., 8.HUSSARS.,	GAUCHE WOOD.	30·11·17
2 LT. BENTLEY, H.L., 2.R.F.,	SAILLY-SAILLISEL.	28·2·16
BDR. CLAYTON, W.H., R.F.A.,	NEAR YPRES.	21·8·17
BDR. TAVERNOR, E.H., R.G.A.,	EPEHY.	26·9·18
L/CPL. HAYWOOD, J.G., 1/5.S.STAFFS.	VERMELLES!	17·8·17
L/CPL. KILBOURNE, F., 7.N.STAFFS.	BAGHDAD.	11·3·17
PTE. ASKEY, J., 2.W.RIDING.,	NEAR ARRAS.	30·8·18
PTE. BARNES, C.W., 18.WELCH.,	NEAR BETHUNE.	17·4·18
PTE. DAVENPORT, F., 8.K.S.L.I.,	NEAR SALONICA.	18·9·18
PTE. DAVENPORT, T., 1.K.S.L.I.,	MORVAL.	26·9·16
PTE. HEDGES, W.C., 10.GLOSTER.	HULLUCH.	25·9·15
PTE. HODSON, J., 13.K.L'POOL.,	MAILLY MAILLY.	15·10·16
PTE. JAMES, J.M., 16.R.WARWS.,	FRICOURT.	26·1·16
PTE. KIRK, J., 25.NORTH'D F.	NEAR CROISILLES.	28·3·18
PTE. WARD, J.H., 1.C.GDS.,	VERMELLES.	17·10·15
PTE. WARD, J.T., 8.E.YORKS.,	TRONES WOOD.	24·7·16

DIED OF WOUNDS

2 LT. BENTLEY, G.W., R.F.C.,	GENEVA.	13·1·16
BDR. LEWENDON, J., R.F.A.,	NEAR YPRES.	22·9·17
PTE. CHEADLE, R.H., 7.BUFFS.,	VALENCIENNES.	12·4·18
PTE. CHEADLE, W., 8.K.S.L.I.,	NEAR SALONICA.	13·1·18

DIED

L/CPL. CHEADLE, E., R.A.F.		14·3·19
PTE. DAINTY, S., 1/5.N.STAFFS.		2·3·19
SPR. SNAPE, F., R.E.		9·10·17

The War Memorial at Sandon, Staffs, with information on those remembered

13

wounds, died of illness or were wounded. It also lists how many honours were awarded and how many served in the different theatres of war.

It can also seem a mystery as to why some men are named on a particular memorial and others are not. There are cases of brothers where only one is listed on the local memorial. Why this happens is not always clear. The parents or widow of one of them may not have wanted their name on the memorial, particularly if he had been reported missing and there was still hope that he would return. Or it may simply be that although born in that parish and living there as a child, he had latterly been living and working somewhere else and could well be recorded on another town's memorial.

So bearing in mind all these inconsistencies how do you start to track down the memorials with your relative's name on?

Locating War Memorials

Even before visiting the places where your relatives lived, the best starting point is to look at the Imperial War Museum's War Memorial Archive (formerly The UK National Inventory of War Memorials)
www.ukniwm.org.uk
This is a free on-line archive that holds details of the whereabouts of war memorials in the UK, Channel Islands and Isle of Man, which commemorate all wars and peacekeeping. So far they have recorded over 60,000 war memorials including many of the more unusual types which so often get overlooked. At present the names on the war memorials have not been listed but the Imperial War Museum have started a major project to have a searchable on-line database of the 850,000 First World War names they already hold to mark the Centenary of the First World War, 2014-18. Following this they will release names for other wars and conflicts. Until the on-line version is available you can contact them for a manual search of the records. IWM London, Lambeth Rd, London, SE1 6HZ. Tel 020 7416 5000.

On a font (Offchurch St Gregory's)   Inside a Lych Gate (Temple Balsall)

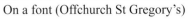

On an individual plaque by a tree
in a Memorial Park (Coventry)

Various types of War Memorial

War Memorial Projects

Within the last few years numerous projects have been taking place by local history groups and individuals to record and research the names on war memorials and these have increased rapidly in the run-up to the centenary of the First World War.

Books

Many books have already been published and it is a good idea to check the libraries or record offices close to where your ancestors lived for any copies of books written about local war memorials.

The War Memorials Trust, a charity that works for the protection and conservation of war memorials across the UK, lists a large selection of books about war memorials at
   www.warmemorials.org/bibliography
in its Learning section. There are also publishers of military books that include books specifically about war memorials. Some of these publishers are listed at the end of this book.

War Memorial Websites

There is an increasing trend for war memorial projects to have their own websites and you could well find a relative listed on one of these. If the town or village you are looking for is not listed on the Imperial War Museum's list then first take a look at the Roll of Honour website
   www.roll-of-honour.com
This is an on-going project run by volunteers and covers hundreds of war memorials throughout the various counties of the UK, mostly World War One and World War Two but also some pre-1914 wars. There are photographs of the majority of memorials, with the names and military details of those recorded on them.

There is also a list of regional war memorial websites on The Imperial War Museum's War Memorial Archive website
   www.ukniwm.org.uk

in their Links section. They are listed under England, Northern Ireland, Scotland and Wales.

Some websites cover large areas of the country such as the North-East War Memorial Project, which aims to cover every war memorial between the river Tweed and river Tees, in the historic counties of Northumberland, Newcastle-upon-Tyne and Durham
www.newmp.org.uk
or the West Wales War Memorial Project which covers three counties – Carmarthenshire, Ceredigon and Pembrokeshire
www.wwwmp.co.uk
Other websites just cover a particular county, town or village and whilst some of these just list the memorials in a particular area with the names as inscribed, most are on-going projects. Research is being undertaken into each individual name with the findings and photographs of the men where possible put on-line. Sometimes a very detailed military history is given as well as details of family and local links. Some take the research even further and look at the history and effect of war on their town such as the Burnley project
www.burnleyinthegreatwar.info
There are however many more websites than those listed by the Imperial War Museum. A simple internet search on the town, village or county of your ancestor together with the words "war memorial" may well find you a website by a local history group or an individual. These websites quite often give links to the books they have produced or links to other projects taking place in that area.

For example, typing 'Buckinghamshire war memorials' into Google leads to the Buckinghamshire Remembers website that gives details of seventeen books about war memorials in that county on the website
www.buckinghamshireremembers.org.uk
A similar search for a particular town or village, such as Raunds in Northamptonshire, may lead you to the relevant website
www.raundswarmemorials.org
From here your journey may just be beginning as each site may give you links to many other related websites for war memorial projects either completed or underway.

As mentioned earlier, cities often have rolls of honour and these can contain thousands of names. Wells Cathedral in Somerset houses a roll of honour in St Martin's Chapel containing 11,300 names of all those born in Somerset who fell in The Great War as well as all those, though not Somerset born, who lost their lives while serving in county units. Photographic reproductions of the Memorial Book are at the British Museum and the Castle Museum in Taunton whilst a downloadable version can be found on Roy Parkhouse's Genealogy Site at

www.parkhouse.org.uk

Similarly the Scottish National Memorial in Edinburgh has the names of nearly 150,000 Scottish casualties from the First World War, over 50,000 from the Second World War, and the campaigns since 1945 including the Malayan Emergency, the Korean War, Northern Ireland, the Falklands War and the Gulf War. The names are contained in books that are on permanent display at the Scottish National Memorial within the walls of Edinburgh Castle. An on-line search of the Scottish Roll of Honour can be done at

www.snwm.org/website/frames.html

By searching these on-line projects you may well come across one of your relatives but you may also be able to track them down through memorials at their place of work, the school or university they attended or the social and sporting clubs they belonged to.

Workforce War Memorials and Rolls of Honour

Large companies encouraged their employees to join up in the First World War or released staff already serving in territorial forces to rejoin their regiments with an assurance that their jobs would be held for them until their return. Inevitably many did not return and so war memorial plaques and rolls of honour were created and displayed in their places of work. Many of these can now be consulted on-line and examples are listed in the following sections.

Railways

The railways were a major employer in the UK at the time of the First World War, with the country split into different regions. After the war they erected large monuments such as those at Euston Station for the London and North Western Railway, the Midland Railway Memorial in Derby, and the North Eastern Railway in York commemorating the thousands of men who died.

The National Railway Museum launched a database in November 2012 listing over 20,000 railway workers who died in World War One. It combines information from items in their archive and library collections and the Commonwealth War Graves Commission giving names, rank, military number, rail department, railway occupation, address, information on families, war memorial and date of death. The list also contains 4,500 references to photographs which are available to view on the open shelves of Search Engine, the museum's library and archive centre at the National Railway Museum in York.

www.nrm.org.uk/RailwayStories/worldwarone.aspx

Some regional railways also have their own websites and here you may find extra information. The Midland Railway gives details of 7,531 employees who had joined the armed forces by 18th November 1914.

www.midlandrailwaystudycentre.org.uk

Their web page 'For King and Country' is searchable by surname or station. The search results, like the National Railway Museum database, gives the person's position on the railway and which department they worked for, but also adds whether they were killed or died of wounds or disease, were reported missing, were prisoners of war, wounded in action or invalided home, or rejected by military authorities as medically unfit.

The Great Western Railway had 25,479 employees join his Majesty's Forces in the First World War which represented 33% of the company's staff. The number of war dead was 2,524. After the war, large framed rolls of honour were displayed in several stations across their region and some can still be seen today. Taunton railway station has an original one whilst the one at Leamington Spa is a replica which was dedicated in 2005 after the original was lost. (See overleaf.)

The Great Western Railway WW1 Memorial in Leamington Spa

Photographs of these casualties, taken from the Great Western Railway magazines, can now be viewed on Flckr. You can find a link in the Related Resources section of the National Railway Museum website
www.nrm.org.uk/RailwayStories/worldwarone.aspx

Post Office (Royal Mail)

In 1914 the Post Office was one of the biggest businesses in the world. Tens of thousands of Post Office workers fought in the war and over 8,500 were killed.

The British Postal Museum and Archive has a searchable catalogue of all the war memorials on Royal Mail premises which cover Mail Centres, Post Offices, Sorting Offices, Delivery Offices and Administration buildings at
www.postalheritage.org.uk/page/collections
Royal Mail is thought to be the second largest custodian of war memorials in Britain, behind only the Church of England.

A search has to be undertaken under place, so you would need to have some idea of where your relative worked. Some of these post office memorials have had the names transcribed whilst others are just photographs of the memorial. There is currently no name search available.

Civil Service

Many civil servants were on active service in the forces whilst other did vital work at home. The Department for Business Innovation & Skills (BIS) war memorials web pages are dedicated to the memory of over 300 staff from BIS predecessor departments who were killed in action or died in war. Their searchable website has entries for both World Wars and links to other Civil Service memorials.

www.dti.gov.uk/warmemorial

Councils often erected war memorials in their town halls and offices. In 1922 the London County Council published a book called 'Record of Service in the Great War 1914-18 by members of the Council's Staff'. This covered all their departments including the London Fire Brigade, Parks, Tramways and Education amongst others. It gives a short military history of everyone who served with an indication of those who died and can now be viewed on-line via the family history website

www.ancestry.co.uk

This is a subscription website with a free fourteen day trial period, for which you must provide a credit card before committing to a regular payment, although you may find you can access this for free at your local library or record office.

Banks and Insurance Companies

Many banks produced rolls of honour and war memorials to their employees. The Royal Bank of Scotland Group cares for over 300 war memorials in properties across the UK and has produced a book of remembrance which records the names of members of staff of its British constituent banks who lost their lives during the First and Second World Wars and the Korean War. The information from the contemporary rolls

21

of honour and war memorials has been supplemented by information from staff records where these were available. A digital version of the book of remembrance can be downloaded from the war memorials and remembrance page of the RBS heritage hub at

heritagearchives.rbs.com

Likewise insurance companies have also produced websites and

www.aviva.com/about-us/heritage

covers all the insurance businesses that are now part of Aviva plc. It can be searched for employees who died and those who received honours in both World Wars together with prisoners of war or civilian internees in World War Two. Some have quite lengthy biographies and a photograph. They also have an interesting section of letters sent home from the front which were reproduced in staff magazines.

Industry

Increasingly employer's rolls of honour are being put on-line, some freely available and others on pay-per-view sites. At **www.findmypast.co.uk** you can search more than 1,900 names in a listing of Oldham companies and the men working for those companies who served in some capacity during World War One. On the same site there are rolls of honour from some 724 companies and institutions from Manchester including The Cooperative Wholesale Society Ltd, Manchester Corporation, the Calico Printers' Association Ltd and the Manchester Ship Canal Company.

Many memorials are still in situ in offices and factories throughout the country, such as the one illustrated, to the four men from the Drawing Office of the Willans and Robinson Engineering Works in Rugby who lost their lives in the Great War.

At Port Sunlight on the Wirral there is a magnificent war memorial to the employees of Lever Brothers companies throughout the world. Over 4,000 men fought in World War One and the names of 503 casualties are inscribed upon the memorial together with 117 from World War Two. In addition, the names of all who served and their war records are commemorated in a book in a cavity in the memorial with copies in Christ Church, Port Sunlight and the Lady Lever Art Gallery.

Memorial from Willans and Robinson Ltd, Rugby

Mining

If you know that your ancestor was a miner try an internet search on the collieries in the area where they lived. Some list all those who enlisted whilst others just list those who died.

Examples include Easington Colliery in County Durham. Their war memorial commemorates the 198 deaths from both World Wars as well as one death from a recent conflict. See

www.ww1-yorkshires.org.uk/html-files/easington-colliery.htm

for details of these men.

Similarly the Ryton & District War Memorials Project,

www.rytonwarmemorials.org.uk

again in County Durham, covers several memorials in an area where collieries were the main source of employment.

In Scotland, the Scottish Mining website

www.scottishmining.co.uk

gives the names from the United Collieries Limited Roll of Employees on active service, 1914-1919. The list gives the names, colliery and regiments of over 2000 employees of the company who served in the First World War. Of these men 289 were killed in action or died of wounds.

Shops and Department Stores

Even shops and department stores had their own war memorials. Those for the firms of J. Sainsbury and Marks & Spencer can be viewed on-line from the Roll of Honour website **www.roll-of-honour.com,** via their Database page, which lists those who died in the Second World War. The database for J. Sainsbury lists employees who were inscribed on a memorial in the entrance hall of the Administration Offices of Stamford House in Southwark, whilst the one for Marks and Spencer has been taken from the book published by Paul Bookbinder entitled "Marks & Spencer The War Years 1939-1945". This lists the surname, first forename and any other initial and the particular office of Marks and Spencer where they were employed.

If your relative worked for a small local business or factory you may find mention of them in business records or rolls of honour that have been deposited in local record offices, museums or libraries.

Schools and Universities

Many schools have their own rolls of honour or memorial books. Some larger schools built memorial chapels following the First World War such as that at Rugby School erected in 1922 to commemorate nearly 700 former scholars who fell in The Great War, later adding 350 after the Second World War. The *Rugby School War Register* which contains the names and services of pupils of Rugby School 1914-1918, together with lists of casualties and honours up to April 1921, has now been scanned and digitised. It can be purchased on CD or as a digital download from
www.anguline.co.uk
who also offer scanned materials from other schools and sources.

Increasingly schools are adding details of their war memorials and rolls of honour to their own websites such as that of Oundle School at
www.inmemories.com/RollOfHonour/oundleschool.htm

The school your relative attended, whether in a town or village, may have had its own handwritten roll of honour to former pupils and it is worthwhile searching local museums and records office for any that have survived. Likewise Sunday School and Bible Class teachers would often compile a roll of honour such as the one for St Barnabas Church in Kenilworth that is displayed on the wall in the church and lists the names of 36 former members of the Church Lads' Bible Class who died in the First World War. You may find such rolls of honour still in the church or deposited in local archives.

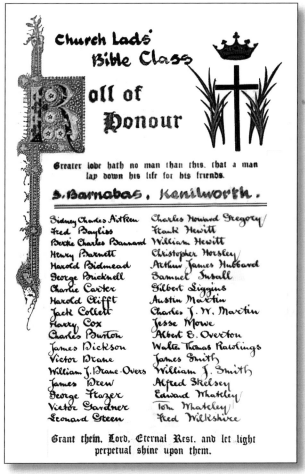

St Barnabas Church Roll of Honour for World War I

Universities are beginning to put their war memorials on-line. The one for Christchurch, Oxford

www.chch.ox.ac.uk/cathedral/memorials

is an excellent site for both World Wars and contains biographical details. Balliol College Oxford has photographs of their War Memorial Book on Flickr. As well as a biography of Raymond Asquith, the prime minister's son, you will also find the college servants listed such as Arthur Sidney Blay, a bedmaker, who was killed in 1917 in France.

The precise link is

www.flickr.com/photos/balliolarchivist/sets/72157625232059789

However, you may find it more quickly by typing 'Balliol College War Memorial Book' or even 'Balliol memorial' into Google. It is often surprising to find how a suitable combination of search words can lead you directly to your desired destination.

Social & Sporting Clubs

It is easy to forget that our ancestors also belonged to social and sporting clubs and many of these had rolls of honour.

Working Men's Clubs

These often included the names of all their members who served in the war as well as listing those that fell. Many of these are still in club premises but may be listed on the IWM War Memorial Archive website

www.ukniwm.org.uk

Friendly Societies

Large numbers of men at the beginning of the 20th century belonged to Friendly Societies. Before the development of government and employer insurance services they were a means of obtaining help in times of illness or unemployment. One of these societies was The Ancient Order of Foresters and as a way of commemorating those who gave their lives in the First World War, they instituted a War Memorial Benevolent Fund,

26

with the aim of supporting widows and orphans. Over 150,000 Foresters had served in the armed forces, of whom over 12,500 had been killed. Local Districts and Courts subscribed to their own physical memorials and Rolls of Honour and accounts of these are in their archives. For example the Newport Pagnell branch in Buckinghamshire sent 290 members to war, 47 of whom did not return. They were recorded on a memorial at the town hall. See

www.aoforestersheritage.com

Freemasons

If your ancestor was a Freemason have a look at the The Masonic Great War Project:

www.masonicgreatwarproject.org.uk

This is a searchable database of Freemasons who took part and died in the First World War. There are over 3,000 names, and in many cases there is considerably more information available than the summary shown in the search facility. This extra information can be obtained via the website from the United Grand Lodge of England.

Sports clubs

Football, cricket, golf and tennis clubs often have their own memorials to those who died in both World Wars. Although many of these have been lost over the years there are still some on local premises and new memorials are being erected such as those put up in recent years at the football clubs of Everton, Brentford and Charlton Athletic. A starting point for a search for sports club war memorials would be on the Imperial War Museum website **www.ukniwm.org.uk**. By putting the name of the sport in the keyword box you can filter down to specific memorials.

The Marylebone Cricket Club at Lord's Cricket ground hosts a series of war memorials, with details on the Roll of Honour website

www.roll-of-honour.com/Middlesex/Lords.html

The Scottish War Memorial Project

www.warmemscot.s4.bizhat.com

lists several golf club memorials and there are details of rowing club memorials on the North East War Memorial project webpage.

Not exactly a sport, but was your ancestor a Church Bell-ringer? There is a Great War Memorial Book of Church Bell-Ringers on display in a bookcase on the way up to the ringing chamber at St Paul's Cathedral, London. This covers bell-ringers throughout the UK and gives name, parish in which he gave his service as a bell-ringer before joining the forces and also that of the Society, Guild or Association to which he belonged. There is now an on-line version on the Central Council of Church Bell Ringers website.

www.cccbr.org.uk/rolls

Research is currently under way to find more about each individual.

World War Two Memorials

Most of the sources discussed so far have been connected to World War One memorials. While 703,000 British service men and women died in that war, 382,600 died in World War Two. To commemorate the newly fallen, many communities extended their existing memorials by adding a second list, usually shorter than the first. In the picture on the opposite page you can see the red sandstone war memorial in the churchyard of the village of Christleton in Cheshire. It was originally erected for the 36 men who lost their lives in the First World War with their names engraved into the stone. After the Second World War a separate metal plaque was added at the base of the memorial naming the 19 men who lost their lives in that conflict.

In the small village of Aldwincle in the county of Northamptonshire, 11 men died in the First World War and their names are placed on two sides of the six-sided memorial, to the left and right of the central dedication. Just one man fell in the Second World War and his name is engraved on the previously empty face to the right of the First World War lists.

At a national level, there was a fundamental change. The First World War involved huge armies face to face in the trenches in France and Belgium. In the Second World War there was a larger role to be played in the air and at sea.

Christleton (Cheshire)
with the fallen in WW2
placed on a separate plaque

Aldwincle (Northamptonshire)
with the single death in WW2
added alongside the eleven
fallen in WW1

Adding the names of the fallen in WW2 to an existing WW1 memorial

Royal Air Force

The RAF, which was in its infancy in the First World War, came to the fore, with the inevitable loss of thousands of airmen. A perpetual shrine of remembrance is maintained at St Clement Danes in London as the Central Church of the Royal Air Forces. It has over 125,000 names recorded in ten books of Remembrance. Book I pre-dates the RAF and has names of balloonists who served with the Royal Engineers, members of the Royal Naval Air Service, the Royal Flying Corps and RAF personnel up to the outbreak of the Second World War. Books II-IX contain the names of all those who died on service during the Second World War and Book X is from the end of the war in 1945 to the present day. Copies of entries can be obtained on request by contacting St Clement Danes, Strand, London WC2R 1DH.

www.raf.mod.uk/stclementdanes

There are several national RAF memorials which were erected after the Second World War. The Air Forces Memorial at Runnymede commemorates by name over 20,000 airmen and women who were lost in the Second World War during operations from bases in the United Kingdom and North and Western Europe, and who have no known graves. They served in Bomber, Fighter, Coastal, Transport, Flying Training and Maintenance Commands, and came from all parts of the Commonwealth. The names are inscribed on panels in a courtyard according to country and squadron.

The Battle of Britain London Monument on the Victoria Embankment, unveiled in September 2005, has bronze plaques with the names and ranks of the 2,937 airmen who took part in the Battle of Britain in the period 10th July to 31st October 1940, including 544 who lost their lives during the Battle and a further 795 who were to die before the end of the war.

The names of all the Battle of Britain airmen are now available on-line

www.bbm.org.uk

with biographies and often photographs of those who died.

The county of Lincolnshire was home to more World War Two airfields than any other in England and Lincoln Cathedral is home to the Airmen's Chapel which houses three memorial books containing the names of

The Battle of Britain London Monument

25,611 Bomber Command aircrew, many of whom died flying from the county.

You may find rolls of honour to specific squadrons in different places around the country. In Leicester Cathedral there is the Roll of Honour to those who died whilst serving in No.7 Squadron RNAS or No.207 Squadron Royal Air Force. It is in a glass topped case in the south aisle of the Cathedral, and can now be viewed on-line

www.207squadron.rafinfo.org.uk/rollofhonour/default.htm

Navy

The Second World War involved the Royal Navy to a far larger extent that the First World War and the losses of sailors was much higher. The naval memorials which had been built after the First World War in Plymouth, Chatham and Portsmouth were now extended. These large obelisk memorials commemorate sailors who died at sea and have no known grave. The Plymouth Naval Memorial which also bears the names of sailors from Australia, South Africa and India commemorates 7,251 sailors of World War One and 15,933 of World War Two. Those for the First World War are on panels affixed to the obelisk's base with the names of the dead arranged by year of death. Those for the Second World War are on panels set into the surrounding wall again by year of death. The memorials at Chatham and Portsmouth contain thousands of names set out in a similar manner to those at Plymouth.

Merchant Navy

Merchant shipping was essential to the wartime efforts as ships were needed to carry food, raw materials, troops and equipment. At the outbreak of World War Two every available ship, regardless of age or condition, was pressed into service. During this war some 50,000 allied merchant seamen lost their lives, of whom over 32,000 were British.

The Tower Hill Memorial in London was unveiled in 1928 to almost 12,000 Mercantile Marine casualties from the First World War who have no grave but the sea. Following the Second World War this was extended in the form of a semi-circular sunken garden and commemorates nearly 24,000 British seamen and 50 Australian seamen listed on its walls. The memorial stands on the south side of the garden of Trinity Square, London, close to the Tower of London. The Memorial Register may be consulted at Trinity House Corporation, Trinity Square (Cooper's Row entrance), Tower Hill, London EC3N 4DH which will be found behind the Memorial. Tel 020 7481 6900.

Civilians

We must not forget the thousands of civilians that died in World War Two. There is a Roll of Honour to the Civilian War Dead in St George's Chapel, Westminster Abbey which commemorates 67,092 civilians of the Commonwealth whose deaths were due to enemy action 1939-1945. The books are kept in a case just outside the entrance to St George's Chapel at the west end of Westminster Abbey. One volume is always open on display and pages are turned periodically. Specific entries can be seen by arrangement with the Dean's Verger (preferably with advance notice). Copies of entries can be obtained from the Commonwealth War Graves Commission at 2 Marlow Road, Maidenhead, Berkshire, SL6 7DX (a charge is made). Another copy of the Roll is held by the Imperial War Museum and can be consulted by appointment in the Museum's library.

Post World War Two Memorials

For those who lost their lives since World War Two, the Armed Forces Memorial at the National Memorial Arboretum now has an on-line searchable roll of honour on the Veterans UK website
www.veterans-uk.info/afm2/index.php
This currently provides information for those who died more than two years ago. The Armed Forces Memorial Project has two further elements which are, or will be, sited in London. A memorial in Westminster Abbey commemorates all those who have died in conflicts throughout the world since the Second World War. Rolls of Honour, similar to those for the Royal Air Force held in the Church of St Clement Danes, are being prepared and, when complete, will be kept in the Church of St Martin-in-the-Fields for the Royal Navy and in the chapel of the Royal Hospital Chelsea for the Army. These will list all those who have died in service since the end of the Second World War regardless of the cause of death. They are to be written on vellum by calligraphers and bound into books.

By using all these sources and doing your own research both on the ground and via the internet you should be able to find one of your relatives on at least one war memorial and can now start researching their military background including where and when they died and the part they played in a particular war.

RESEARCHING THE NAMES
ON WAR MEMORIALS

You may well find that your relative has already been researched by someone else and the findings published. However it is always best to check this research for any mistakes and omissions. First of all you must confirm that the person listed on the war memorial is in fact your relative. With common names and sometimes just a surname and initial it is often difficult to tell if you have the right one. The normal family history research route needs to be taken initially which will include

Census Returns

The 1891, 1901 and 1911 censuses are particularly useful for researching relatives who fell or served in the First World War as you may find your relative living in the place where his name is on a memorial. Censuses are available at local record offices, the National Archives at Kew, or via subscription websites such as Ancestry:
www.ancestry.co.uk
or Findmypast:
www.findmypast.co.uk

Civil Registers

If you do not already have the birth or marriage certificates of your relative it is worthwhile buying these. A birth certificate will confirm the names of parents and a marriage certificate will give the wife's name and if it took place during wartime may also give the regiment her husband belonged to. These can be bought from the General Register Office or from district registrars, but in order to obtain them you must search the General Register Office (GRO) indexes. Full indexes are available on Ancestry or Find My Past and many libraries and record offices hold them on microfiche. You can also see them on FreeBMD
www.freebmd.org.uk

although not all years are yet complete. The indexes will give you the information needed to order a certificate and they can be ordered via the GRO website

www.gro.gov.uk/gro/content/certificates/faqs/birth-death-marr. asp

If your relative died at home from sickness or wounds received in action you should be able to obtain a death certificate in the same way as described above. You can also buy death certificates of overseas military deaths even if killed in action overseas. Find My Past has an index and the certificates are available from the General Register Office. However be aware they may not give much information, and are unlikely to give an accurate cause or place of death.

Parish Registers

You can also consult the parish registers for where your relative lived and these should be available at local record offices. Here you may find details of a baptism or marriage, again with possible details of the regiment that your relative belonged to. It is also worth looking at burial registers. If a soldier was injured or taken ill overseas he may have been brought back to England, died here and been buried in the local churchyard or cemetery, whilst other soldiers died of illness at home before they could be sent abroad. There should be a burial entry for them in the church register which may be at the local record office, but if it was a burial in a cemetery their records are usually still with local councils.

Once you have details of your relative such as date of birth, parents' names and where they lived you should turn to the free on-line records of the Commonwealth War Graves Commission

www.cwgc.org

to cross-reference them with military service details.

The Commonwealth War Graves Commission (CWGC)

This was established in 1917. Its duties are to mark and maintain the graves of members of the forces of the Commonwealth who were killed in the two World Wars, and to build memorials to those with no known graves. It has a casualty database which lists the names and place of commemoration of the 1.7 million men and women. It also records details of the 67,000 Commonwealth civilians who died "as a result of enemy action" in the Second World War.

The database at **www.cwgc.org** is searchable by name and gives individual details of

- ◆ name,
- ◆ initials,
- ◆ rank,
- ◆ regiment,
- ◆ unit,
- ◆ age at death,
- ◆ date of death,
- ◆ service numbers (except for officers),
- ◆ cemetery or memorial details,
- ◆ additional information, such as details of parents, wife, and home address.

However, only 65% of the casualties have next of kin recorded because not all the 'Final Verification' forms sent to the last known address of a casualty's next of kin were returned.

The dates covered by the CWGC are for those who died between 4th August 1914 and 31st August 1921 and 3rd September 1939 and 31st December 1947, so you may find someone recorded on a war memorial but because they died after the cut-off dates they will not be in the Commonwealth War Graves lists.

Some families turned down the offer for a CWGC headstone as they provided a memorial or gravestone privately. The photographs opposite show a private grave for a young airman and a Commonwealth War Graves Commission gravestone placed within the family plot, where the deceased soldier has already been named on the family gravestone.

A private gravestone for a fallen airman

A Commonwealth War Graves headstone on a family grave

The greatest problem with the CWGC website is finding the correct record as there are many servicemen with the same name and initials. So if you already know the regiment they served in and have an idea of their age or date of death this can help identify the correct man.

On their website is a link to the War Graves Photographic Project
   www.twgpp.org
which is a joint project with the CWGC and enables families and researchers to obtain a copy of the photo of a grave or memorial for a small fee. There is a search facility to see if a photograph is available and if so it can be sent electronically or by post.

Soldiers Died in the Great War

Even if you find your World War One relative on the Commonwealth War Grave Commission website it is a good idea to cross reference it with the information from a database known as 'Soldiers Died in the Great War'.

This is available online via Ancestry, Find My Past or in CD format at some Record Offices and libraries. The database has been compiled from lists published by HMSO in 1921 on behalf of and by authority of the War Office, of those who died during the Great War. It includes over 703,000 individuals, both officers and 'other ranks', and gives similar information to the Commonwealth War Graves website, but also includes where the soldier was born, where he enlisted and also where he was living when he enlisted.

It may often give a man's full name instead of just initials. For example in my own research one man was listed on our local war memorial as H L Bidmead. This is how his name appears on the Commonwealth War Graves Commission database, but, by looking at Soldiers Died in the Great War, I was able to establish that his name was in fact Harry Lloyd Bidmead and it also gave me his place of birth.

There is a similar database to Soldiers Died in the Great War for the Second World War entitled **Army Roll of Honour 1939-1945,** again available on Ancestry, Find My Past or in CD format in record offices and libraries. This is less helpful than the World War One database as it only gives the county as the birthplace and place of residence.

38

Absent voters lists

Another useful resource for World War One, and one quite overlooked, are the Absent Voters Lists of men in the armed forces prepared for the General Election in Britain in 1918. These usually recorded the man's regiment, number and rank or rating at the time, as well as his home address. Although they have not all survived they are held at County Record Offices or local history sections of main libraries in the area where the man lived in 1918. There is information about existing lists at **www.1914-1918.net** including details of those that are now on-line, some of which are free, whilst others are to purchase or pay-per-view.

Towards the end of the Second World War on 31ˢᵗ January 1945, two electoral registers known as the Civilian Register and the Service Register were compiled for each Parliamentary Division. These are not as useful as the earlier registers as they only contain the qualifying address and an indication of whether the voter was a serviceman, sailor or war worker.

Newspapers and printed sources

Before delving into military service records, one of the most fruitful searches you can make is to look at newspapers, particularly local ones, as they can be an excellent source of information for casualties, particularly for the First World War. Newspapers printed obituaries, lists of missing and wounded soldiers, details of medal awards and citations and often photographs. If you are searching for a death in the newspapers you may have to look for several months after the event as many deaths were not reported for quite some time.

You may also find, particularly in smaller towns, copies of letters submitted by the families of men who wrote home or from officers sadly reporting a man's death. These letters were more commonly printed in the first two years of the First World War, in part because newspapers became smaller with the increasing shortage of paper, but also because the government did not wish to report the appalling losses of men at the front, particularly after the Battle of the Somme in 1916.

James Harris, the Kenilworth postman, can be followed throughout his war-time experiences by newspaper reports and letters he sent home to his family and post office colleagues as he graphically describes life in the trenches. The local newspaper also published a poem he sent to his wife (see opposite). After nearly four years at the front the newspaper reports his death, killed in action in February 1918.

You may also find your relative mentioned in local newspapers in the reports of Military Service Tribunals starting in 1916. When the compulsory enlistment of unmarried men between the ages of 18 and 41 was introduced, applications were allowed to be made to the tribunals for exemption from the call-up on grounds of occupation, hardship, faith or moral belief. Many employers appealed on behalf of their workers. Some men were given conditional exemptions and appealed again several months later, but the tribunals became increasingly strict with the heavy losses of men at the front and the need to replace them. Inevitably some of those who were made to go and fight lost their lives. A Kenilworth farmer in early 1917 pleaded to keep his 18-year old waggoner saying he was urgently needed until the spring planting and summer cultivation had been finished. His application was refused. His worker was called up later that year, taken a prisoner in early 1918 and not released until January 1919. His health was broken and he died in 1920; as a consequence, his name appears on our war memorial.

Some newspaper reports of military tribunals do not mention specific names whilst others give full names. You may also find surviving military tribunal papers in your local archives. If your relative came from Middlesex you may strike lucky with a database which has recently come online listing 8,000 men who appealed to tribunals against their conscription. These are downloadable for free until 2024 from **www.nationalarchives.gov.uk/records/middlesex-military-service-appeal-tribunal.htm**

You should find copies of local newspapers on microfilm in local libraries or record offices. The British Newspaper Library which used to be at Colindale in London has now closed but is being remodelled to create a new News & Media Reading Room at St Pancras. Here it will be possible to access microfilm and digital collections.

Private James Harris
Injured
Kenilworth Advertiser
14 November 1914

KENILWORTH MAN WOUNDED.

Private J. Harris, 2nd South Staffordshire Regiment, has been wounded in the right arm and also in the right thigh, and has been taken to hospital in Calais.

Private Harris was a postman in Kenilworth, and as a reservist was called up immediately on the outbreak of hostilities, proceeding immediately to the front.

Return to the trenches
Kenilworth Advertiser
10 July 1915

LETTER FROM PRIVATE J. HARRIS.

Private J. Harris, a Kenilworth postman who is back again in the trenches after recovering from wounds, writes to his fellow postmen thanking them for gifts of tobacco. He says: "The position of the lines we are holding now is very dangerous as we are only 25 yards from the Germans, and we exchange bombs all day and night. I am sorry to say we had 30 casualties, three killed and 27 wounded in the four days we were in the trenches. The ground between us is undermined by both sides, and we blew up one of the German trenches the other day and killed 15 and buried 25 in the debris, so you see we are playing them at their own game. I am glad to say that their sap heads and mines are not so accurate as ours, for ours do twice the amount of damage."

From the front
Coventry Herald
19 November 1915

KENILWORTH SOLDIER'S LETTER.

A PARODY ON "SING ME TO SLEEP."

Private J. Harris, whose home is at 42, Henry Street, Kenilworth, has sent his wife a letter from the trenches in France, where he is serving with "D" Company of the 2nd Battalion South Staffordshire Regiment. Writing under date of November 15th he says: "Just a few lines to you to let you know that I am going on all right. . . . We are in the trenches again for a few days and it is very cold and damp, but never mind, we must be satisfied with being alive and pretty fair in health, only for a cold." continued ...

... continued

At the end of his letter Pte. Harris, who is well-known in Kenilworth by reason of the fact that he was formerly a postman here, adds a parody on the well-known song "Sing me to Sleep." with a request that it should be passed on to the "Coventry Herald." This soldier's song has not a cast-iron libretto, but is adapted by individual soldiers to suit their own circumstances, and as Pte. Harris seems to possess quite a journalistic gift of giving the thing a "local flavour" we print his version of the parody below:

"Sing me to sleep, where bullets fall,
Let me forget the war and all.
Damp is my dug-out, cold are my feet,
Nothing but bully and biscuits to eat.
Sing me to sleep where bombs explode,
And shrapnel shells are a la mode.
Over the sandbags helmets you find,
Corpses in front of you, corpses behind.

Far from the trenches I long to be,
Where German snipers can't pot at me.
Think of me crouching where worms do creep,
Waiting for someone to put me to sleep.
Sing me to sleep in some old shed,
A dozen rat holes around my head,
Stretched out along on my waterproof,
And dodging the raindrops from the roof.

Sing me to sleep where camp fires glow.
For over the top we've got to go,
Dreaming of home and nights in the West.
Somebody's boots resting on my chest.
Far from Henry Street I seem to be.
Lights of old Kenilworth I'd rather see:
Think of me crouching where worms do creep,
Waiting for sergeant to say 'Next relief!'"

Killed in Action
Kenilworth Advertiser
2 March 1918

KENILWORTH AND THE WAR.

PTE. JAMES HARRIS KILLED IN ACTION.

Mrs. Harris, of 4, Henry Street, Kenilworth, received the distressing news on Monday last that her husband had been killed in action in France. The deceased had last written on the 2nd of February that he was due to stay in the trenches for four more days. He was killed on the following day. Private Harris was an old soldier who had served 18 years in the army and on reserve. He was called up on the outbreak of war, and was wounded three months later, in the first battle at Ypres, and except for the period of incapacitation following that wound and two short home leaves he had served 3½ years in France. He belonged to the 2nd South Staffs. Regiment, with which he had experienced numerous battles and engagements. He was last home four months ago. The news has been confirmed by a comrade, who found in the deceased's coat a money order for Mrs. Harris, which he sent on to her. There are three children, the oldest being seven years only. At the outbreak of war Private Harris was a postman at Kenilworth, his round being Bubbenhall.

Information about a soldier in the local newspapers

The British Library are in the process of putting thousands of newspapers online at

www.britishnewspaperarchive.co.uk

and some of these now cover the years of the First World War. The index is free to view but you have to pay to view the entire content.

National newspapers such as the Times, The Scotsman and Irish Times also published casualty lists, details of medal awards, officer promotions and deaths and obituaries of officers. These are now all searchable online, the Times being available for free in some libraries and record offices whilst the Scotsman and Irish Times are pay per view sites.

The London Gazette, which is freely available on-line at

www.london-gazette.co.uk

published military appointments, promotions, awards and some citations.

Second World War newspapers, because of increased censorship, tended to give less details of casualties and did not publish letters sent home, but it is still worthwhile searching them and again you should be able to find copies at local libraries and record offices.

Church Magazines and Parish Records

Church magazines are another valuable resouce and are often deposited in local record offices. Rolls of Honour appeared throughout the war years and sometimes the vicar would write in detail about a parishioner who was active in the life of the church when he died (see opposite).

It is also worthwhile looking through parish record collections at local record offices. These may include the printed programmes or order of service for the unveiling of a war memorial and usually list those on the memorial, although they may not give you any more detail than the name as it is inscribed. Sometimes you can come across real gems amongst parish records. I have found instances of vicars keeping scrapbooks about all the men from their parish who went off to war, with details of those injured or killed and sometimes including letters and newspaper cuttings. Many record offices now have online catalogues so you may be able to track down something like this before you visit the office.

St. Nicholas', Kenilworth.

List of Those who have Given their Lives for their Country.

"Greater love hath no man than this, that a man lay down his life for his friends."

"Lord, all-pitying Jesus blest, Grant them Thine eternal rest."

Alfred Aitken
Sydney Charles Aitken
Ernest Thomas Ashmore
Bertie Charles Bannard
Walter John Barber
Henry Barnett
Harold C. Bates
Sidney Butler
Charlie Carter
Cyril Wm. Carter
Jack Cashmore
William Chaloner
Reginal Dennis Clive
Merwyn Colomb
Harry Cox
William John Drane-Overs
Donald Ewen
Frank Edward Feneran
Ernest Alfred Frazer
Victor Gardner
John Garratt
Albert Edward Gillam
Leonard Green
James Harris
William Hewitt
Harry Hincks
Christopher Horsley
Arthur James Hubbard
Samuel Insall
Guy E. Kidd
Ernest Letts
Gilbert Liggins
Charles Matthews

Alfred Miles
George Mitchener
Harry Mitchiner
John Charles Morgan
Jesse Mowe
Albert Overton
William Jacob Parkin
Francis Plant
Walter Thomas Rawlings
Alfred Reeves
Edward Reeves
Leonard H. Reeve
James Reynolds
William Robertson
William Robertson
Harold Ruddock
Arthur Sawyer
Constance Seymour
Laurie Seekings
James Smith
William James Smith
Alfred Skelsey
Edgar Thompson
Jim Tookey
Reginald Carlyon Tweedy
Trevor Tweedy
Norman Ward
William Watson
Edward Whateley
Tom Whateley
Dudley White
Fred Wilkshire
William Wilkshire

N.B.—This list includes the 'names of 22 of our old Sunday Bible Class members.

Roll of Honour in the Kenilworth St Nicholas Magazine, April 1918

St. Nicholas' Parish Magazine.

Norman Ward.

One of the most promising of our young men has been taken from us. It was only a few weeks ago since he came to make his Communion before starting for the Front. He had finished his training, and had just received his Commission in the 11th Royal Warwicks. After the service he found his way to the Vestry—"Good-bye, Vicar, I'm off to the Front at last. The 'big push' is on, you know." Scarcely three weeks had passed when we heard that he had been killed in the attack. He was moving his men to a safer position when he was struck down.

He leaves behind him a record of Christian service which ought to inspire all who knew him. His splendid work in the organization of the Sunday School will be remembered; he was a master of detail, and possessed the gift of leadership in a marked degree. He was a faithful member of the King's Messengers of the S.P.G., and did an equally fine work in organising ways of serving the Missionary cause. Our sympathy goes out to the parents who have lost their only son. They have at least this consolation, that his life, though short, was a very full one.

Entry by the Vicar in the Kenilworth St Nicholas Magazine, September 1916

43

MILITARY SERVICE RECORDS

Having hopefully found your relative in the records of the Commonwealth War Graves Commission or an article in the local newspaper, you can now turn to service records to get a fuller picture of their military history. You will need to have made a note of the regiment and service number to help locate these.

If your ancestor was an army officer their career is usually fairly easy to discover from official army lists, the first of which was published in 1740. Since 1754 they have been published regularly as annual lists (1754–1879) and quarterly lists (1879–1922). Since 1939 they have been classified and are still with the Ministry of Defence and are not available to the public. The vast majority of Army lists up to 1913 are still at the National Archives at Kew but many have now been published on CDs or are available on subscription family history websites such as
www.thegenealogist.co.uk

Boer War

The National Archives at Kew
www.nationalarchives.gov.uk
holds records for soldiers of the Boer War some of which have been digitized and can be downloaded for a small fee. They are also available on the following pay-to-view websites.
The Register of the Anglo-Boer War 1899-1902 is at
www.casus-belli.co.uk
and is a database that lists men and women who served in the British Imperial Forces during the war in southern Africa including soldiers, sailors and nurses. To date there are over 272,643 entries which includes a fully revised and corrected casualty roll of over 59,600 records. This is now also available at Find My Past.

Ancestry also has a Boer War collection which documents 20,000 British soldiers who died in the conflict and a further 23,000 who were injured. The database has each soldier's name, rank, regiment, and date and place of the injury or death, as well as the details of the 78 soldiers

44

awarded the Victoria Cross, the highest military honour.

The Roll of Honour website

www.roll-of-honour.com

also has many links to sources of information about the Boer War.

World War One Service Records

The National Archives at Kew holds a vast variety of servicemen's records for the First World War. You can visit in person and view some of these on microfilm, but as many of its records are now online it is worth checking their online catalogue before making a visit.

www.nationalarchives.gov.uk

Army

The majority of the seven million who served in World War One were in the British Army and all soldiers had a service record. Unfortunately only about 30% of these records survived bombing in 1940 which caused a fire in the building where they were stored. These are often referred to as the 'Burnt Records' and many are just fragments or damaged pages.

Officers

Records for officers who served in World War One were amongst those destroyed by bombing in 1940 and of those that survived many were 'weeded' out resulting in mostly miscellaneous information remaining in the records, mainly concerning claims for pensions and allowances. The records for most British Army Officers are available at the National Archives although they are not yet online. Files for 140,000 officers who left the Army before 1923 are available in Collection WO339. These are men who served as officers of the regular army (including those on temporary commissions for the war).

You can also find the service records of almost 78,000 Territorial Army Officers including those holding a temporary commission in Collection WO374, but again these have been 'weeded' in a similar fashion.

Non-commissioned officers and other ranks

Collection WO363 (known as the Burnt records) at the National Archives contains the records for non-commissioned officers and other ranks who served in WW1, and did not re-enlist in the Army prior to WW2, and were either killed in action, died of wounds or disease, or survived and were demobilised at the end of the war. These can be viewed on microfilm at the National Archives, but are also available online through Ancestry under *British Army WW1 Service Records 1914-1920*.

If you manage to find a full set of Service Papers that have survived these will include:

◆ the name of the soldier,
◆ service number,
◆ regiment,
◆ age,
◆ birthplace,
◆ occupation,
◆ marital status,
◆ physical description,
◆ next of kin,
◆ a full account of military service including promotions, postings and medical history.

In the case of soldiers who were killed or died you may find letters to their next of kin about surviving personal belongings or the issue of medals.

Collection WO364 (known as the Unburnt Records), and also referred to as the Pension Records, contains the service records of non-commissioned officers and other ranks who were discharged from the Army to pension, either as a regular at the end of their period of service but more often discharged because of wounds or illness. Again these can be viewed on microfilm at the National Archives or online through Ancestry under *British Army WW1 Pension Records 1914-1920*.

Both the soldier's service and pension records should be searched when looking for a soldier.

The exception to these are the Guards regiments who maintained a separate set of records which survived the Blitz. These are available via the Regimental Archivist for the relevant regiment – i.e. Grenadier, Coldstream, Scots, Irish or Welsh. Enquiries should be sent to Wellington Barracks, Birdcage Walk, London, SW1E 6HQ.

British Army WW1 Medal Rolls Index Cards, 1914-1920.

Even if none of your relatives' documents have survived in the Service or Pension Records you can search the Medal Rolls Index cards. These were created to keep a single record of a soldier's medal entitlement. Every soldier who served abroad was awarded at least one campaign medal. You can view them at the National Archives, Collection WO372 on microfilm, download them from their website for a small fee or view them on Ancestry. The cards have slightly different formats but all contain name, rank, unit or units in which they served, service numbers, and sometimes the first operational theatre in which they served and the date they landed overseas, as well as the medals to which they were entitled.

Officers had to claim their medals, so you often find address details on their cards, but ordinary soldiers were automatically sent theirs. In the case of both officers and soldiers who died in the war the medals were automatically issued to their next of kin, so again you may find the name of the next of kin and an address on the card.

The difficulty with the Medal Rolls Index Cards is the sheer quantity (approx 4.8 million people) which makes searching on a common name quite difficult unless you know the regiment and service number. Sometimes a soldier may have more than one medal card particularly if they changed regiments.

If the medal card indicates that your ancestor received other medals, such as a Victoria Cross (VC) or a Distinguished Conduct Medal (DCM), the citations for these were originally published in The London Gazette and can be viewed online at
www.london-gazette.co.uk
Sometimes it may be problematic trying to find the right entry. When looking for the 1915 citation for Kenilworth man Lance-Corporal Leonard Henry Reeve, serving with the King's Royal Rifles, as a last

resort I wrote to the Great War Forum at
1914-1918.invisionzone.com/forums/index.php
and had an almost immediate response from an expert that took me straight to the desired page (shown opposite). I was also given a helpful tip that I might shortcut the whole business by simply putting the right information into Google. By putting **Reeve 11935 "London Gazette"** into the search engine, it immediately came up with the right page. It doesn't always work but is worth a try!

Silver War Badges

Another source worth searching, which can be particularly useful if a man's service records have not survived, are the Silver War Badge rolls in Collection W0329 at the National Archives. The initials SWB on a medal card tells us that that the man is on the Silver War Badge roll. The Silver War Badge was awarded to all military personnel who had served at home or overseas during the war and had been discharged. This was most commonly on medical grounds because they were no longer physically fit, having been wounded or taken seriously ill and they may have subsequently died at home. The War Badge rolls give details of the man's date of enlistment, number, rank, regiment, unit at time of discharge, date and cause of discharge and whether he had served overseas. Sometimes his age is given. A database can be found on the Ancestry website in their WW1 Military collection entitled *UK, Silver War Badge Records, 1914-1920.*

Prisoners of War

Many men died whilst prisoners of war or after returning home.
    Records of 7,703 British Army Officers who were POWs between 1914 and 1918 can be found on Find My Past
    www.findmypast.co.uk
This gives first and last name, rank, service, section, date they went missing and date they were repatriated and additional notes such as death in captivity.

Distinguished Conduct Medals—*Continued.*

Regimental No.	Rank.	Name.	Corps.	Action for which commended.
6346	Serjeant ...	Rees, H.	1st Battalion, Royal Irish Rifles	For conspicuous gallantry and ability at Neuve Chapelle on 10th March, 1915, in handling his platoon, on one occasion going under very heavy fire to his Company Commander for orders. Again on 12th March he kept his platoon well in hand during very heavy shelling. Serjeant Rees' conduct throughout has been most gallant. He was severely wounded on 12th March, 1915.
11935	Lance-Corporal	Reeve, L. H. ...	1st Battalion, King's Royal Rifle Corps	For conspicuous gallantry and devotion to duty, when he, with other men, captured an enemy's trench. His Officers being wounded early in the morning, he held it from 8.15 a.m. to 2 p.m. in spite of a heavy fire and severe losses, refusing to leave until ordered to do so by a wounded Officer.
9291	Bandsman	Regan, G. P. W. ...	2nd Battalion, Leinster Regiment	For great courage and devotion to duty on 14th March, 1915, in dressing the wounded under a very heavy fire.
6847	Acting Corporal	Reid, J.	1st Battalion, Cameron Highlanders	For conspicuous gallantry at Bixschoote on the 22nd October, 1914, when, by his courage and devotion to duty, he retained, with his men, a hold on a trench, although under a very heavy machine gun fire from two directions. Subsequently he went back and brought up ammunition along a road swept by machine gun fire, and thereby prevented any advance by the enemy.
1290	Lance-Corporal	Rendall, J.	2nd Battalion, Welsh Regiment (attached to 170th Company, Royal Engineers)	For conspicuous gallantry on the 1st April, 1915, when, at about 1 a.m., under a bright moon, he went out in front of the advanced trenches and brought in a wounded man from within 40 yards of the German trenches, being fired on heavily the whole time.
24503	Corporal ..	Revell, E. G. ...	2nd Signal Company, Royal Engineers	For conspicuous gallantry and resource in charge of a telephone detachment throughout the campaign. On several occasions he volunteered to go out and repair telephone lines under shell fire. On the 10th March, 1915, at Cuinchy, the wires between Brigade Headquarters and Battalions being frequently cut by shell fire, he mended them, thus maintaining telephonic communication without a break throughout the day.
9937	Corporal ...	Rickard, S. G. ...	"C" Air Line Section, Royal Engineers	For conspicuous zeal and devotion to duty when carrying out his work as Chief Linesman with his Company.

Part of a page from The London Gazette list of DCMs

War Diaries

One of the most useful resources for building up a picture of what a particular battalion was doing on a given day are the War Diaries.

Army units were required to keep a War Diary which was a daily record of operations, intelligence reports and other events. One copy was sent to the War Office and that copy has now been transferred to the National Archives (Collection WO95) where they are available to view in their original form. There are over 10,000 diaries and some of the most frequently requested ones have now been digitized and are available to download for a small fee from the National Archives website. More digitized diaries will be published online throughout 2014 as part of their centenary programme.

The other copy was kept by the unit and some of these are now in regimental museums or county record offices where you may view them.

The content of war diaries can vary greatly and although officers are regularly mentioned and often named, other ranks are rarely included although very occasionally there are casualty lists. Even if your relative is not mentioned by name, when the battalion was involved in a major offensive an hour by hour report was given, often very graphically, and this can give you an insight into the circumstances of just what happened to your soldier relative and his comrades.

Soldiers Wills

Soldiers were encouraged to make a will before departing for the frontline and these handwritten wills were kept in their pocket service books.

English held First World War soldiers' wills have recently been digitised and can be searched for online at
https://probatesearch.service.gov.uk
Each will costs £6, but be aware that you may not always get a complete will as sometimes soldiers only left letters or brief instructions.

The will of James Harris, the Kenilworth postman, is a brief handwritten will written on a page in his pocket service book, saying that in the event of his death he gives the whole of his property and effects to his wife.
50

This was dated 24th October 1916 and after his death in February 1918 would have been extracted from the service book.

Scottish soldiers wills have been digitised and are available at the National Records of Scotland
www.nrscotland.gov.uk
These will appear on the ScotlandsPeople website in the near future.
www.scotlandspeople.gov.uk
The National Archives of Ireland has also digitised its WW1 soldiers' wills and these are freely available at
http://soldierswills.nationalarchives.ie/search/sw/home.jsp

Navy

Fortunately Naval records for WW1 were not destroyed in the Blitz and are now held in the National Archives
www.nationalarchives.gov.uk
Many of these collections have now been digitised and put on-line on their website, whilst others have been digitised in partnership with commercial publishers. The on-line records at the National Archives are downloadable for a small fee and the most useful for you to search are probably the following:

The Royal Navy ratings' service records 1853-1923 (ADM 139 & 188)

These give information of ratings which includes: year of birth, town and country of birth, names of ships served on with dates of joining and discharge from each ship, notes made about character and ability, physical appearance such as hair and eye colour, height and tattoos.

The Royal Naval Division Service Records 1914-1919 (ADM 339)

The service records of ratings and officers in the Royal Naval Division (RND) during the First World War. The RND, which was formed in September 1914, fought on land alongside the Army. It consisted of personnel brought together from the Royal Naval Reserve, Royal Fleet

Reserve, Royal Naval Volunteer Reserve, a brigade of Royal Marines, Royal Navy and Army personnel.

About 50,000 service records of men who served in the Royal Naval Division are available to search and download from their catalogue. These service records are now also available on Find My Past.

Royal Navy Officers' service records (ADM 340)

The service records of officers who joined the Royal Navy between 1756 and 1931.They include service records for commissioned officers joining the Navy up to 1917 and warrant officers joining up to 1931. They also feature the records of Royal Marines officers commissioned between 1793 and 1925.

Naval Casualties records 1914-1919

are now available on Find My Past. Almost 45,000 Royal Navy sailors lost their lives in the Great War and these records give details of naval other ranks deaths. Information given includes their full names, rating, number, branch of service, name of ship or unit, decorations, date and cause of death, location of cemetery and grave reference, and name and address of the relative notified of the death.

Air Force

The Royal Flying Corps (RFC) was in existence from 1912 to 1918. In July 1914 the RFC's naval wing was detached to form the Royal Naval Air Service (RNAS). On 1 April 1918 the two services were merged again to form the Royal Air Force (RAF).

The service records of RFC airmen who died or were discharged before the foundation of the RAF in 1918 were kept with the British Army personnel records, so you need to do a search as given for the Army records. There are also over 26,000 members of the RFC and nearly 27,000 men of the RAF listed in the medal rolls index cards and again you should search as for the Army medal rolls.

Someone who served in the RFC or RNAS as well as the RAF may have service records in more than one place.

The service records of RNAS ratings who served before the foundation of the RAF were kept with the Royal Naval seamen's service records. You can see on the National Archives website the Register of Seaman's Services 1853–1923 and download the records for a small fee. You will also find Naval medal rolls 1793-1975 on Ancestry.

If an RNAS rating or RFC airman continued to serve in the RAF after April 1918, his record would be kept with RAF service records. These are at The National Archives at Kew,
www.nationalarchives.gov.uk.
You can search by the name of the airman in the series AIR 79 via the Discovery catalogue.

Royal Air Force officers' service records for 1918-1919 are also available in series AIR 76, and contain records of over 99,000 men. Although the records were created from the inception of the RAF in April 1918 they include retrospective details of earlier service in the Royal Flying Corps or Royal Naval Air Service, where appropriate. They are also downloadable for a small fee.

A further useful resource for RAF personnel is the on-line Flight Magazine 1909-2005. The Flightglobal Archives explores 100 years of aviation history as it appeared in the original pages of Flight Magazine which have been digitally scanned and are fully searchable for free. The magazine lists RAF casualties, lists of those missing and also promotions.
www.flightglobal.com

Women at War

Many women became military nurses in the First World War and inevitably some died or were killed.

The majority served in the Queen Alexandra's Imperial Military Nursing Service (QAIMNS). Their records which are downloadable for a small fee are at the National Archives
www.nationalarchives.gov.uk
in class WO399 for nurses who served in the Queen Alexandra's Imperial

Military Nursing Service (QAINMS), the Queen Alexandra's Imperial Military Nursing Service (Reserve) QAIMNS(R) and the Territorial Force Nursing Service.

There are also campaign medal records (1914-1920) which again are downloadable for a small fee. You will find them under British Army Medal Index Cards 1914-1920 on the National Archives website. Class WO372. If you use the keywords 'Nurse', 'Voluntary Aid Detachment' or 'Queen Alexandra's', as well as providing a surname this will help your search.

Other women worked for the Voluntary Aid Detachments (and were known as VADs). Members were trained by the St John Ambulance Brigade and served alongside all branches of the armed forces. For a service record of a person who served in a Voluntary Aid Detachment from 1914-1920 you should contact the British Red Cross Museum and Archives, 44 Moorfields, London, EC2Y 9A.

www.redcross.org.uk

They hold a series of indexes recording the service details of personnel who worked throughout both world wars.

Record cards may include the dates of service, the nature of the duties performed, the detachment the individual belonged to, the institutions and places where the individual served, and any honours that may have been awarded. In addition, there are indexes for personnel who served in military hospitals, who were trained nurses, and who received the war medal.

There is just one woman named on Kenilworth War Memorial and that is Constance Emily Mary Seymour, the youngest daughter of Lord and Lady Ernest Seymour, who was a probationer nurse with the Queen Alexandra's Imperial Military Nursing Service. She worked at the Kenilworth Red Cross Hospital, which was opened in the Parochial Hall, but later joined the staff of the Cambridge Military Hospital at Aldershot and then the Connaught Military Hospital. At this hospital she caught measles from a patient and died in February 1917. She is buried in the Aldershot Military Cemetery and was given a military funeral. Her nursing records do not appear to have survived.

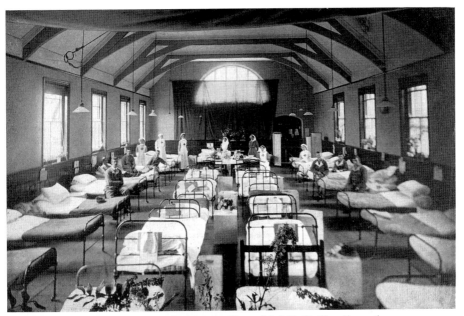

Red Cross Hospital in the Parochial Hall, Kenilworth

The Grave of Constance Seymour
Aldershot Military Cemetery

World War Two Service Records

Service records for both men and women of the British Army, Royal Navy (RN), Royal Marines (RM), Royal Air Force (RAF) and Home Guard personnel of World War Two are still in the custody of the Ministry of Defence (MOD) until they are opened to general public access at the National Archives.

The information that is held on an individual varies depending on which Service they served with, when they served and the length of their service. Sometimes little or no information may be held. Records can be released for a fee of approximately £30 although there may be a lengthy wait for this service. Information and the different forms you need can be found at

https://www.gov.uk/requests-for-personal-data-and-service-records

For those where death was in service in World War Two you can expect to find surname, forename, place of birth, age, date of birth, date of death, service number, rank, the units in which he/she served, the dates of this service and the locations of those units, and details of World War Two campaign medals.

Prisoner of War Records 1939-1945

If your ancestor was captured by the enemy you should be able to find information on

www.findmypast.co.uk

They hold 166,037 records of prisoners which gives name, rank, regiment, army number, camp number, POW number, the type of camp and its location and extra notes where applicable.

British Army Unit War Diaries 1939-1945

These can be found at the National Archives. They give details of invasions, battles, secret operations and daily activities of army units (as recorded in unit war diaries). However, they have not been catalogued and only a few are digitized.

Nurses

The Ministry of Defence (MOD) hold the service records for the Royal Army Nursing Corps (QARANC), the Queen Alexandra's Royal Nursing Service (QARNS) and the Royal Air Force Nursing Service (RAFNS) for World War Two.

As with other service records details of these and how to apply for them are at
https://www.gov.uk/requests-for-personal-data-and-service-records

Voluntary Aid Detachments Nurses (VADs)

During the Second World War, VADs came under the jurisdiction of the military despite being civilians. Their service records can be found by writing to British Red Cross Museum and Archives, 44 Moorfields London EC2Y 9A. Further information is on their website at **www.redcross.org.uk**

The Home Guard

Information contained within the Home Guard records is very limited. It normally consists of one double sided A4 sheet of paper (Army Form W3066) containing personal details on enlistment and very little else. No details are held of the duties performed by an individual during his service. Again you can download forms from
https://www.gov.uk/requests-for-personal-data-and-service-records
and there is a non-refundable administration charge of £30. It should be noted that a considerable proportion of searches for Home Guard records prove to be unsuccessful.

For more details of other sources concerning the Home Guard, ARP Wardens and the Royal Observer Corps see

Raymond, Stuart A. *The Home Front* 1939-45, The Family History Partnership 2012.

Post World War Two Service records

The service records of deceased Service personel who died post World War Two can also be applied for via the Government website
https://www.gov.uk/requests-for-personal-data-and-service-records
However for a period of 25 years following the date of death of the subject and without the consent of the next of kin, the MOD will disclose only:

surname, forename, rank, service number, regiment/corps, place of birth, age, date of birth, date of death where this occurred in service, the date an individual joined the service, the date of leaving, good conduct medals (for example, Long Service and Good Conduct Medal), any orders of chivalry and gallantry medals awarded.

After the 25 year period, and if it is held, the MOD will also disclose without the requirement for next of kin consent: the units in which he/she served, the dates of this service and the locations of those units, the ranks in which the service was carried out and details of campaign medals awarded.

There is a £30 administration fee.

FURTHER RESOURCES

If you want to explore your ancestor's military history in greater depth, and learn more about the war they took part in, you may find some of the following resources useful including forums where you will find experts, both professional and amateur, all willing to help and freely share their knowledge on different aspects of war.

The Imperial War Museum
www.iwm.org.uk
covers conflicts involving Britain and the Commonwealth from the First World War to the present day.

The National Archives
www.nationalarchives.gov.uk
holds thousands of war-related documents as well as audio and podcasts.

The National Army Museum's Templer Study Centre offers visitors an opportunity to explore in depth the campaigns, personalities and social history of the British Army.
www.nam.ac.uk

British Military Nurses for both World Wars are included in the Scarlet Finders website.
www.scarletfinders.co.uk

Boer War

Details of the battles with illustrations and maps can be found at
www.britishbattles.com

The Boer War has a forum at
www.victorianwars.com

First World War

The Long, Long Trail will tell you all you want to know about soldiers, units, regiments and battles of the British Army of the First World War.
www.1914-1918.net

The Great War Forum is linked to The Long, Long Trail at
1914-1918.invisionzone.com

The Western Front Association (WFA)
www.westernfrontassociation.com
is the website of the WFA which was formed to further interest in The Great War of 1914-1918. There are branches throughout the country.

The BBC has a World War One website with many articles and podcasts at
www.bbc.co.uk/ww1

The British Library has a website with over 50 articles about World War One written by leading experts
www.bl.uk/world-war-one

Second World War

The BBC World War Two People's War is an archive of 47,000 stories and 15,000 images.
www.bbc.co.uk/history/ww2peopleswar

Traces of War links to sites and places of interest related to the Second World War in Europe and beyond.
www.tracesofwar.com

World War Two has a forum at
www.ww2talk.com

WHAT TO DO WITH YOUR RESEARCH

Having found your ancestor on a war memorial and researched their history what do you do with the results?

You will obviously want to share your findings with your immediate family but you might also consider publishing a booklet or starting a website. You could write an article for your local newspaper or for a newspaper from the area where your ancestor lived, or you might share your research with local history groups and societies such as The Western Front Association.

You could also contribute to an on-line project being run by the Imperial War Museum, **Lives of the First World War,** which is an interactive digital platform bringing material from museums, libraries, archives and family collections together in one place. This can be seen as a permanent digital memorial.

www.livesofthefirstworldwar.org

Some people expand their research into the actual physical war memorial, looking at who designed it and how the money was raised to build it. You might also research all the names on the memorial not just your family ones. This is how I started my interest in war memorials as part of a millennium project for my local family history group. See

www.kenilworth-war-memorial.org.uk

If a war memorial you are researching is in need of repair have a look at the War Memorials Trust:

www.warmemorialstrust.org

This is a charity that works for the protection and conservation of war memorials in the United Kingdom and offers advice and information as well as running grant schemes for repair and conservation.

You can report concerns about a war memorial to War Memorials Online:

www.warmemorialsonline.org.uk/memorials

and can add information and photographs about the condition of a memorial as well as comments on its history or those commemorated. You can create links to other websites and contribute to creating a record of those commemorated to ensure it is known who they were if a memorial is lost, damaged or stolen.

In Scotland the Government have set up a scheme named the Centenary Memorials Restoration Fund (CMRF) and made £1 million available for repair and conservation works to war memorials in Scotland during the centenary of the First World War. This is to be administered by Historic Scotland. Advice and guidance notes can be found at
www.warmemorials.org/grants-scotland

FURTHER READING

The following is a select list of books to help you research your military ancestors

The Crimean War 1854-56, Phil Tomaselli, 2006, Federation of Family History Societies

Tracing Your First World War Ancestors, Simon Fowler, 2003, Countryside Books

Tracing Your Second World War Ancestors, Simon Fowler, 2006, Countryside Books

The Second World War 1939-1945, Phil Tomaselli, 2011, Pen & Sword Family History

My Ancestor was in The British Army (Second Edition), Michael J Watts and Christopher T Watts, 2009, Society of Genealogists

My Ancestor was a Royal Marine, Ken Divall, 2008, Society of Genealogists

My Ancestor was a Merchant Seaman, Christopher T and Michael J Watts, 2011, Society of Genealogists

Tracing Your Air Force Ancestors, (2nd edition), Phil Tomaselli, 2014, Pen & Sword Family History

My Ancestor was a Woman at War, Emma Jolly, 2014, Society of Genealogists

The Home Front 1939–1945, Stuart A Raymond, 2012, The Family History Partnership

The following is a list of book publishers selling books on general military history that may include books written about specific war memorials throughout the UK.

Naval and Military Press
www.naval-military-press.com

Pen & Sword Books
www.pen-and-sword.co.uk

The History Press
www.thehistorypress.co.uk

Countryside Books
www.countrysidebooks.co.uk

On-line bookshops can be found at

The Family History Partnership
www.thefamilyhistorypartnership.com

The Society of Genealogists
www.sog.org.uk

The National Archives
bookshop.nationalarchives.gov.uk

The Imperial War Museum
www.iwmshop.org.uk/category/947/Books

The Western Front Association (WFA)
www.westernfrontassociation.com/online-books-dvds.html